A SELF HELP BOOK FOR THOSE THAT DON'T KNOW

THEY DON'T KNOW
TDK

Tips for Lack of Life's Basic Skills, Knowledge and
Manners for Pre-Teens, Teenagers, Young Adults,
and Parents

By Regina Shaw Small

Table of Contents

Forward

For many years, I have noticed the lack of basic knowledge and respect shown by our youth and young adults today and how many lack the basic skills typically provided by parents to help them survive and become wholesome adults. Some might say having basic knowledge is the same as having common sense or 'Mother Wit' (i.e., common sense). Don't get it confused, having book sense or being book smart is one thing, but having common sense is totally different. Many of our ancestors who were uneducated, lived solely on common sense which came natural and allowed them to survive. To a certain point I agree, but many people **Do Not Have a Clue** when it comes to **Common Sense** ......they don't get it and most just don't know. While some struggle with basic common sense, it is a natural way of life for others. Having common sense is a good thing for those who are able to naturally command knowledge and able to survive, but having common sense does not provide one with the basic skills for survival.

Many parents today rely solely on teachers to train their children and provide them with the basic skills and manners that should be provided by parents. I <u>totally disagree</u> with parents relying on teachers to do their job. With each new generation, we are losing our children. Parents should be their children's first teacher. Parents 'Where are you'? Initial training and parenting should start at home, but in many cases today it does not, which is what prompted me to write this book 'They Don't Know – Tips for Lack of Life's Basic Skills, Knowledge and Manners'.

Home Economics and Life Skills Courses use to be a mainstay in our public school systems across the country, but has become extinct in many systems in a time when basic skills are badly needed. Home Economic classes reinforced and filled the gaps with life skills not received at home. These courses should be a constant in our schools and can be reinstated by petitioning your local School Board through the Parent Teacher Association (PTA), Parent Teach Student Association (PTSA) or the Parent Teacher Organization (PTO). Get involved and know the curriculum and course work provided at your local community school.

My initial thoughts for this book did not include biblical references, but my life is so entwined, centered around and based on the Bible for encouragement, biblical references could not be excluded.

This book is dedicated to my parents, the parents of a lifetime Thelma and Alonzo Shaw Sr. both deceased, who worked hard to raise a family of five children; four daughters Evon, Marlene, Doristine and me (Regina) and one son Alonzo Shaw Jr. They were God fearing, stern, fun loving, and allowed us enough rope to independently venture out to learn and grow, but still maintain parental control. They didn't play when it came to raising us, where hard work and knowing your responsibility was major. We were respectful to our parents, ourselves and others. Talking back, sassing, or talking under your breath was not tolerated.

My Mother was a stay at home Mom, a very good cook and the disciplinarian, while Daddy was the sole provider who provided all of our basic needs and some of our wants. He retired from the Firestone Tire and Rubber Company after 33 years. Daddy was also a good cook specializing in gourmet items such as Coubion (Pronounced Coo-bee-Yon or Coo-bee-On) or Fish Head Soup a Cajun dish, other delicious spicy soups and stews. He also made the best rice and bread pudding in the world. At times, Daddy would steam whole blue crabs, a rarity in Tennessee. We weren't poor, but as kids we thought we were rich because we had loving parents who exposed us to much and raised us to be responsible people. Daddy served our country in the U.S. Army and he fought in World War II (WWII). He retired from the Army as a Master Sergeant, where he served with the Army Corps of Engineers.

Every 5-6 years, Daddy would come home with a new car for us to check out and Mama would test drive it for her approval. We had love and nothing else mattered. We had a well-rounded childhood growing up. We were exposed to a lot of different activities such as trips to the zoo, the circus, band trips, church activities, Girl Scouts and Boy Scouts, the annual Cotton Carnival, the County Fair, and summer trips to overnight camp for two weeks. Our hard work paid off and we were rewarded for doing our chores such as cleaning the house every weekend, dusting, polishing silver, washing dishes, hanging clothes outside on the clothes line, ironing clothes, polishing the hardwood floors after waxing them with socks by sliding across the floor for fun, emptying the trash cans, washing the car, defrosting and cleaning the freezer, cutting the lawn and much more. We never complained about doing our chores, because we always made it fun by singing and dancing.

Many of the chores that I performed as a child do not exist today, such as defrosting the freezer and hanging clothes outside on a clothes line. Most have been redirected by technological growth. We now have frostless freezers, dishwashers and clothes dryers.

Back in the day, one rule in our house was, do not ask to go anywhere until all of your chores are completed. My Mom was stern, whenever we were out of order, all she had to do was give us what we termed as "The Look" and we immediately stopped what we were doing and straightened up. Mama often commented to her friends that she didn't need to buy a dishwasher, because she had five dishwashers. She was referring to her five children.

We participated in numerous school and church activities, social clubs, marching and concert band, church choir, Jr. Usher Board, the sunshine band, summer camp in the park, Candy Stripes (i.e., Volunteer Nurse's aide at hospitals), National Defense Cadet Corps (NDCC), Reserve Officers Training Corps (ROTC), Girl Scouts, Boy Scouts, and much more. One thing is for sure, if you joined any activity, you could not quit. Quitting was never an option.

When it was time for family fun, our parents became the kids and they were the best. Our house was the neighborhood gathering house with lots of snacks and kids, mostly boys flocked to our house. Mama could tap dance and she made sure we all knew how to tap, she was also very good at playing all games such Jacks, Jump Rope and Roller Skating. If fact, Mama could "spread eagle on roller skates just as good as any of the boys". Daddy was the practical joker and teaser. All of the kids loved my parents. There was never a dull moment and lots of fun in the

Shaw household. Some Sunday evenings, Daddy would take the family out for a ride and on the way home he would purchase a gallon of ice cream. We would be so excited about the little things. We even took family vacations. I can vividly recall going to visit an Aunt in St. Louis, Missouri and visiting the St. Louis Zoo. Mama and Daddy, thank you for a wonderful childhood. We love and miss you both.

My husband Gleason is also thankful for his parents Nellie and Roman Small both deceased, who also provided a well-rounded childhood and raised him and his siblings to be responsible people as well. His family makeup was almost the opposite of mine, in that, there were four sons; JC, Buford, Gleason, and Norman and two daughters Juease and Geraldine. My Mother in-law Mama Nellie, which she was affectionately called, made sure her children, were equipped with the basic life skills for survival such as showing respect, cleaning the house, ironing, washing dishes, mopping floors, cooking and after school jobs when the time was right. Mama Nellie and Daddy Roman made sure their children understood their responsibilities and were equipped with the right tools for survival. Their children participated in several church and school activities, but team sports was high on their list of activities. Time was also set aside for family fun, but most of all they enjoyed family time together. *Ephesians 6:2 –* "Honor your Father and Mother, which is first commandment with promise".

We thank God for our parents who <u>RAISED</u> and carried us all to the point of being able to fly out of the nest and survive on our own with the basic skills for survival. We are also thankful for being taught from an early age how to respect ourselves and be respectful to others. We love you all and we miss you very much. Those were the good old days.

I hope you enjoy this book as much as I enjoyed writing it and I hope it is a help to someone. Do me a favor, if you learn anything from this book, if only one item, please share your new found knowledge with someone. Pay it forward!

Sincerely,

Regina S. Small

QUICK BASIC CHECKLIST FOR SURVIVAL

- ✓ Always Live a Godly Life.
- ✓ Always Pray Daily.
- ✓ Always RESPECT yourself and others.
- ✓ Always Dress for Success.
- ✓ Always Maintain Good Hygiene.
- ✓ Always Train your Child and Maintain Parental Control.
- ✓ Always Be a Good Neighbor.
- ✓ Always Use Proper English.
- ✓ Always Be a Courteous Driver.
- ✓ Always Communicate with your Child Daily.
- ✓ Never Drink or Text while Driving.
- ✓ Develop a Financial Plan or Budget.
- ✓ Maintain a Balanced Diet and Exercise Daily.
- ✓ Be Gainfully Employed. Do the Work and No Slacking.
- ✓ Be Grateful and Have a Grateful Heart.
- ✓ Help one Another without Expectations. Pay it forward.
- ✓ Do Not give to others what you Do Not want for yourself.
- ✓ Do Not knock each other down. Empower each other. Be supportive and build each other up.

Personal Reflections – Basic Checklist for Survival

1. What are your thoughts about the Basic Checklist for Survival?

2. Are you familiar with every item on the checklist?
   If not, identify the items with no familiarity.

3. Did you learn anything that you did not know?

4. Discuss your thoughts with your family and write your findings.

ADDITIONAL COMMENTS

Chapter 1

Keep God First in Your Life

Chapter 1 - One of the biggest mistakes of our society was made June 25, 1962. On that day it was decided that prayer and the Bible would be removed from our public schools. The decision to remove God from the school system took our protection away from the schools and weaken our conviction for what is good and right. Starting each day with prayer was a wonderful way to kick-start each day. Our children are our future. What are we teaching our children other than what is part of the school curriculum….. hate, racism, and gun violence? We need God in our daily walk more than ever today. To keep us grounded with a God centered life of love, to maintain world peace, keep our children safe, drugs away, and to keep hatred, guns and foolishness out of our schools. Without God nothing is possible, with Him 'All things are possible'. *Matthew 19:26* – "And looking at them Jesus said to them, with people this is impossible, but with God all things are possible".

Do you know God? If not, pray and seek His guidance to get to know Him. *John 3:16* - "For God so loved the world, that He gave His one and only begotten Son, that whosoever believeth in Him shall not perish, but have everlasting life". Do you have a church home that you fellowship with? If you do not belong to a church, pray daily, ask God for guidance in finding a church home to worship. Visit several churches, before you settle on a church home. Be sure to review the church covenant for each church under consideration before you make your final decision, to ensure that you are in total acceptance with the church's binding agreement.

Take your child to church and to Sunday school. **Do not send**

them. Go to church as a family unit. Sunday school is a great start to begin your family's Christian walk. Be available for family discussions to answer any questions that might arise. Remember to keep God first in all things, thank Him daily for blessing and keeping you and your family on the right track. Prayer changes things. Pray consistently. *1 Thessalonians 5:17* – "Pray without ceasing". There are so many activities in the church for the entire family such as; Approved Workmen are Not Ashamed (AWANA) targeted for children, educational field trips, educational classes, church fellowships, adult activities, and individual activities targeted specifically for men, women and singles.

Are you familiar with the three T's of Giving; time, talent and treasure? Be a good steward and find out how in the body of Christ to manage your time, talent and treasure. Incorporating the three T's in your life will enlighten and strengthen you and help maintain a strong family bond. *Haggai 1:7* – "Thus said the Lord of hosts, Consider your ways".

Personal Reflections – 1

1. Do you know God?

   Do you have a personal relationship with God?

2. Do you have a church home?

3. Are you at a place in your life when you need change? Explain?

4. What are your thoughts about this chapter?

5. Did you learn anything that you did not know?

6. Discuss your thoughts with your family and write your findings.

ADDITIONAL COMMENTS

Chapter 2

The True Meaning of Respect

Chapter 2 - *Respect* is defined as a positive feeling or action shown towards someone held in high regard, a sense of admiration for good qualities. Respect is also the process of listening, caring and consideration for others feelings. In order to receive respect or be respected, you must show respect by first respecting yourself. Learn to be a good listener. Listening is an art and a learned behavior. Just because you are a certain age does not mean you know everything, even as an adult. Never think that you know everything because you don't. My parents advised me throughout my adult life until the day they died. I listened intently each time I was advised, even if the information was something I already knew. 'Why', you might ask? Simply because I respected my parents and I valued the words of wisdom they provided.

Respect starts with 'You' and is a common courtesy such as being polite to others. Respect is taught at an early age. It's very difficult to change a person later in life, but it can be done. Practice makes perfect. Consistently repeating a behavior over and over, will eventually become a habit and a natural way of life.

Always say 'Please and Thank you'. Say 'Please' when making a request and 'Thank you' when the request is granted. Greeting someone when you enter a room and not waiting to be spoken to is a common practice. Try it, it won't hurt you. Saying good morning every morning to your family and friends whether you're in a good mood or not, saying **'please'** and **'thank you'**, and **'holding the door'** for the person behind you, are also all common practices. Do you realize 'holding the door' for someone is a simple and a kind gesture? It has nothing to do with the color of your skin? Do not become offended if the person you hold the door for does not thank you. This is a common courtesy. Many will allow a door to close on people following behind them because of their race, 'Stop It'. This is crazy thinking and down-right **STUPID**. You should not see color when it comes to doing the right thing. In fact, others might not hold the door for you. When this happens, guess what…..**they're STUPID too.** Do not stoop to their level, don't be dragged down by the stupidity of others, don't do what others do, think for yourself and do the right thing. There was a phrase popularized years ago, 'What Would Jesus Do…..WWJD'? Think of this phrase when unsure of what to do in all situations. *Do Not Be a Follower. Think for yourself.* Do you remember the Golden Rule? **"Do unto others as you would have them do unto you".** I learned the golden rule in Kindergarten and I often recall it to my memory as an adult.

Another way to show respect on public transportation, in a waiting room or any situation that presents itself. If there is an elderly man or woman standing or a woman expecting a baby, offer them your seat. They might decline, but making the offer is the right thing to do. Also, men offer a woman your seat if she is standing. This is true respect. Honor your elders, you will be an elder one day and paying respect forward ensures that this positive quality is passed on. *Romans 12:10 –* Love one another warmly as Christians, and be eager to show respect for one another".

Never interrupt a person when they are talking, always allow a person to finish what they are saying. This shows respect as well as showing you are interested in what they are saying. If you need to speak, always say **'Excuse me'** before speaking. Never allow your child to interrupt an adult or any person when speaking. This happens way too much because it is allowed. When this happens, immediately correct the behavior. Start by stopping your child and telling them to apologize to the offended person. Tell them to always wait until the person finishes their conversation, before they begin speaking. Back in the day, children were not allowed to sit around adults when having a conversation. They were promptly ushered out of the room or told to exit. I can vividly recall my Mama saying "Go play or read a book, Get out of here". Parents should also teach their child/children to always knock on a door when closed and wait for a response before entering. You cannot teach your child respect if you do not respect yourself and others.

Learn how to apologize and teach your child/children how to apologize, when they have wronged someone. An apology is a form of respect. Once you apologize, you are released from the guilt, worry and baggage and you can move on, it frees you. Receiving an apology has the same affect, no more worry. Saying "sorry" is not a proper apology and borders on disrespect. To apologize, make eye contact with the person receiving the apology and say "I'm sorry or I am sorry" from your heart. The same holds true when someone is apologizing to you, always make eye contact.

Another lost form of respect for children is responding to adults by saying, "Yes Ma'am, No Ma'am and Yes Sir, No Sir". In the south, many children still address adults or their elders with "Yes Ma'am and Yes Sir", but a simple response of 'Yes and No' is mostly used today. Thank God teachers are still addressed properly in school. They are addressed by Ms., Mrs., or Mr. and their first or last name. Typically, teachers write their name on the board the first day of school. Do not allow your children to respond to you or any adult by saying "What" or "Huh", this is disrespectful and totally unacceptable. Although it sounds like a foreign language when I hear the old salutations, I love hearing the **old school** respect. There is never too much respect. Words to remember, 'Please', 'Thank you', 'Good Morning', 'Good Night', 'Yes', 'No', and 'Excuse me'.

Personal Reflections – 2

1. Do you respect yourself and others?

   Do you show respect for your elders (i.e., the older generation)?

2. How can you make a difference when people are disrespected?

3. What are your thoughts about this chapter?

4. Did you learn anything that you did not know?

5. Discuss your thoughts with your family and write your findings.

ADDITIONAL COMMENTS

Chapter 3

Love Thy Neighbor as Thyself

Chapter 3 - Have you ever asked yourself 'What has happened to our neighborhood' or 'where has neighborly spirit gone'? To have a good neighbor, you must be a good neighbor. Periodically, take five minutes to have a conversation, to introduce yourself and get to know your neighbor. A neighbor is the best eyes you can have when you're not at home. Welcome new neighbors to the neighborhood. *Leviticus 19:18* – "Thou shall not avenge, nor bear any grudge against the children of thy people, but thou shalt love thy neighbor as thyself. I am God".

Join your neighborhood or homeowner's association and get involved. Attend neighborhood events, get to know your neighbors by name. Love and help one another.

Personal Reflections - 3

1. Do you know your neighbors?

2. Have you ever had a real conversation with your neighbors?

3. What are your thoughts about this chapter?

4. Did you learn anything that you did not know?

5. Discuss your thoughts with your family and write your findings.

ADDITIONAL COMMENTS

Chapter 4

Parental Guidance

Chapter 4 - The topic of Parental Guidance is a very sensitive subject to me. I love children and it gives me great pain, when I see parents young or old not parenting their children or when a child is totally out of control. Parents remember 'they didn't ask to be born' and not raising children properly or ignoring small issues with your child is not the answer. Ignoring a small issue over time leads to a bigger problem. Stay in control. Seek help when you are not sure of what to do. Contact your Physician, local Community Center or a School Counselor for information and guidance. God gave you the ultimate gift and blessed you to be a parent. Man up and do your job. Children want to be raised, they love guidance because they are learning. Many new and established parents are missing in action by allowing their children to partially raise themselves, while others allow their children to be in total control. It's sad to say, but many people blessed with children are not raising them, while those who are not fortunate to have children would love the opportunity. Remember material things do not equate to love. This is one of the biggest mistakes parents today are making. You cannot buy love. Providing material things should not substitute for loving, properly raising your child and constantly communicating with them. You are in control. Teach and communicate, teach and communicate, teach and communicate is the name of the game.

Some say the trend where there is little to no parental control started when Mother's left the home to join the work force, but this is not the sole reason for the lack of parental guidance. Many working Mothers should be given credit for holding down the fort while raising a family, and a great majority of the Mothers are single. Others say one of the reasons for the lack of parental control is due in part because of the 'Latch Key Child'. Children coming home alone and letting themselves in after school and unsupervised for the most part are raising themselves. Unless, Mom and/or Dad have some very structured checks and balances or some standards in place for their child/children while they are absent, there will be a lack of parental control. There are so many reasons for the huge deficit in parenting, starting with the TV, which is often times used for a babysitter, too much unsupervised TV with no parental controls, too much time for unsupervised video games with no parental controls, cell phones usage, and not enough time for outside playtime or structured activities. Always set aside time for homework. Unsupervised homework time and the lack of parental guidance can lead to poor grades and low self-esteem. Always check your child's homework whether they want help or not. Set a pattern, create a checklist or schedule and make sure all items on the checklist are covered daily to include family time. Allow your child to maintain the checklist, which will help motivate and keep them engaged with the planned structure.

Enroll your child/children in as many activities (i.e., track and field, swimming, basketball, gymnastics, football, cheerleading, tap, girl scouting, boy scouting, English, ballet, financial literacy, sewing and much more) as possible and affordable. Check your local community center or Boys & Girls Club for a schedule of activities. Get involved. Keep your child/children busy. Do not allow them to become bored. Keep their minds moving and challenge them constantly. As a parent, be involved in all activities as a volunteer. Stay abreast of what's going on and be in the know. On rainy days or during inclement weather, limit TV time. Always keep activity books, crafts and games on hand, both educational and fun to fill the void. Inclement weather is the perfect time for family bonding. Be creative. **Ephesians 6:4** – "Fathers, do no provoke your children to anger, but bring them up in the discipline and instruction of the Lord".

Over the years, many of the facts listed have added to our children being out of control. You might ask 'Why don't I have control over my child/children'? The moment you allow your child to make decisions that should be made by an adult, they are raising themselves. This could be the beginning of problems in your household, but not in all cases. Be consistent with your discipline, make a schedule and stick to it. Parenting is actually like being a teacher, you must have a weekly plan. Purchase a board and post the weekly schedule to include, chores, homework, activities, and free time. Discuss the schedule with your children, so that there is complete understanding of the expectations. Children want to be trained, they thrive on learning and being challenged. Stay in constant contact with your child/children's teacher or coach weekly or on a consistent basis. Visit the school often, join the Parent, Teacher, Association (PTA) or the Parent, Teacher, Student, Organization (PTSO), attend meetings, be visible and be known at your child's school. Be a permanent fixture at school and activities as long as you child/children are in attendance at the school. Remember you are the 'Parent' and you are responsible for the nurturing and well-being for your child/children. Get to know the parents of your children's friends. You can assist each other with carpooling, backup parenting/babysitting and provide support in times of need. Your child is not responsible for themselves. You have the final word until their 18th Birthday and sometimes beyond (i.e., college). If you do not care, neither do the educators or coaches. Hug your child every day and tell them you love them. **Listen more, be a good listener.** Let your child know they will make mistakes, but the secret is to learn from their mistakes and not repeat them. Regardless of their mistakes, reassure your child you will always love them. Teach your child that there are consequences for their actions and to always think before they act or respond. Raising a responsible child leads to a responsible adult. Teaching a child responsibility early in life is the pathway that leads to accountability and reliability in school, work habits and everyday life. ***Ephesians 6:1 –*** "Children, obey your parents in the Lord, for this is right". ***Colossians 3:20 –*** "Children, obey your parents in everything, for this pleases the Lord".

Methods for disciplining children varies from timeout, to spanking, to withholding favorite items to talking to them. Find out what works best for you. Discipline is necessary to maintain parental control. Teach your child how to communicate and share their feelings. Some children have a difficult time expressing themselves and cannot communicate with anyone, even their parents. If this is the case, find a responsible adult or guidance counselor to talk to that you or your child are comfortable with and trustworthy. Select a person you trust that you can contact for any situation that will not judge or question you regardless of the situation. Always make eye contact, this means looking directly at the person you are talking to or talking to you. Eye contact is vital when communicating.

Proverbs 22:6 – "Train a child in the way he should go, and when he is old he will not depart from it".

Personal Reflections – 4

1. What does parental guidance mean to you?

2. Do you know where to find help?

3. Are you a good listener?

4. Do you communicate daily with your children and family?

5. Do you spend quality time daily with your children? If so, how much time?

6. What are your thoughts about this chapter?

7. Did you learn anything that you did not know?

8. Discuss your thoughts with your family and write your findings.

ADDITIONAL COMMENTS

Chapter 5

Basic Life Skills - Your Daily Life

Chapter 5 - Certain things in life are typically taught at an early age, but it is never too late to learn and acquire some of the basic skills for survival. Most things in life are not mandatory, but somethings are required for your normal existence in everyday life; such as washing your face, brushing and flossing your teeth and respect for yourself and others. When you rise every morning, makeup your bed every day, eat a good breakfast, get dressed and be on time for any scheduled activities (i.e., work, school or appointments). Just think, what would your life be like if you never washed your face or brushed your teeth? The answer is 'YUCK', don't do it. This is not the way. Take care of yourself!

Some of the basic things in life that you should have been taught when you were a child that positively sets your day in motion, makes you feel good and starts your day off right, such as taking care of your body, eating a good breakfast, exercising, cleansing your body, daily meditation and saying 'Good Morning'. Have you ever noticed that your day seems off or you feel like you are in a fog when you miss your morning ritual, quiet time and/ or breakfast? Breakfast is one of the essential items necessary in jumpstarting your body with the right fuel for the day. That's why teachers always tell their students to eat a good breakfast the day of any formal exam, especially standardized tests, so that your mind is fog free. Starting your day off with quiet time is also essential to some.

Setting a good daily pattern is a positive way to start each day. Nothing is accomplished staying in bed all day and not caring for your body. Your body is your temple, take care of yourself, so that you can take care of your family.

Be an example for your child/children, family and friends. Children do what they see and say what they hear. In other words, if your child/children see's you not caring for your body, they will not care for theirs. Likewise, if your child hears you using profanity (i.e. cussing) all the time, they will use profanity too. Always be a positive example or role model and 'let your little light shine'.

How to make a Bed. To make a bed, you will need a set of sheets appropriate for your bed size, pillow cases and a bed covering (i.e., a blanket, comforter, spread, or duvet cover). *Make up your bed every day*. Start by putting the appropriate fitted sheet size (i.e., twin, queen or king) on your bed. Next, put the top sheet on the bed, and then tuck the foot of the bed first, then tuck the corners and sides. Add a comforter or spread to dress-up the bed and make it fancy. Coordinating pillow shams and throw pillows can be added for the final touch. Remember to change your sheets at a minimum of once a week or at a maximum every two weeks.

Basic table setting. Do you know how to set a table? Did you know that each utensil, plate and glass plays a specific role in a table setting? A properly set table is a beautiful start to a formal or informal family meal, dinner or event. A few things to remember for a basic table setting: 1) Dinner plates should be placed approximately one inch from the edge of the table, 2) the fork should be on the left side of the dinner plate, 3) the knife is placed on the right side of the plate, with the blade facing inward, 4) the spoon is placed to the right of the knife and 5) the napkin is always placed to the left of the fork(s). The napkin should be placed in your lap before you start to eat. All of these utensils should lineup with the dinner plate and be approximately one inch from the table's edge. Additional spoons and forks used for formal place setting are placed next to forks and spoons already in the place setting. Glasses are placed above the plate on the right side and above tip the knife and spoon. Enjoy the pictures of an informal basic table setting from Regina's table pictured below.

Regina's *Basic Table Setting -1 (without a placemat)*

Regina's *Basic Table Setting -2 (with a placemat)*

Do you know when to start eating at an informal/formal affair? Do not begin eating until the Host begins or the food has been blessed. Do you know which fork to begin eating? If there are two forks, always begin with the outside fork. Do you know what each item in an informal/formal place setting is used for? See Regina's table settings in the Basic Table Settings section.

Respondes, sil vous plait (R.S.V.P.) – A common courtesy often overlooked and misunderstood is the RSVP, which is French and translates to "Respond if you please". Many confuse RSVP to mean respond if attending the event, this is not true. In order to assist the host or organizer with planning, you should respond if attending or not attending the event in a timely manner per the invitation. An affirmative (i.e., yes) response, means you plan to attend the event. Do not respond 'Yes' if you do not plan to attend. In most instances, a prompt response is vital for planning when a large number of guests are invited and is very costly. Money is lost when you respond and do not attend. Be supportive of ones wishes. If not attending, please respond promptly by saying or indicating "Regrets only". **NEVER CRASH AN EVENT!** Crashing an event does not have a good look and is very poor taste.

Saying Grace before Each Meal – Early on as a child and in many religions and cultures, we are taught to pause before each meal to give thanks to God by 'Saying Grace', which is a way of expressing our gratitude for the blessing. Some cultures say Grace by quoting scriptures from the Bible, while others express gratitude with their own spoken words. Some sample early childhood Graces taught are below.

An early childhood Grace taught to me and my children;

'God is great and God is good and we thank Him for our food, by His hands we are all fed, give us Lord our daily bread. Amen'.

Another Grace;

'Lord please bless the food we are about to receive for the nourishment of our bodies and bless the hands that have prepared this food I pray. Amen'.

Pray with your Child Each Night – Saying a good night prayer with your child each night is a wonderful way to develop a habit for praying with your child. It is also a good way to find peace and help you and your child settle down before going to bed.

You might remember the following prayer;

'Now I lay me down to sleep, I pray the Lord my soul to keep. May God guard me through the night, and wake me with the morning light. Amen'.

The Lord's Prayer

Our Father who art in heaven, hallowed be thy name. Thy kingdom come. Thy will be done on earth as it is in heaven. Give us this day our daily bread, and forgive us our trespasses, as we forgive those who trespass against us, and lead us not into temptation, but deliver us from evil. For thine is the kingdom, and the power, and the glory, forever and ever. Amen.

Tell your child you love them, hug and kiss them every day and night. Periodic kisses during the day are good too.

Cleaning your Room – If you are blessed to have your own room or even if you share a room, you can show your gratitude by keeping your room clean, making your bed daily and hanging up your clothes. This might sound like a lot, but by doing these simple things daily, it will take less effort to maintain and keep your room clean.

Washing dishes – Another good practice is to wash dishes after every meal. First, teach your children how to properly wash dishes, how much soap to use and the proper water temperature. Make it a habit and house rule that dishes must be washed after each meal or dinner if possible and at a minimum before going to bed. In many households today, dishwashing is nonexistent and has been replaced by dishwashers. If this is the case, teach your child how to load the dishwasher. Never leave or allow dishes to be left in the sink overnight. Washing dishes or loading the dishwasher can be added to the list of daily chores and easily incorporated into your schedule. Maintaining household dishes is a Monday thru Sunday chore. Remember, it takes less effort to maintain dishes if washed after each meal and not allow them to pile up. *Philippians 4:13* – "I can do all things through Christ who strengthens me".

Personal Reflections – 5

1. Are you equipped with life's basic skills?

2. Where did you learn your basic skills?

3. What are your thoughts about this chapter?

4. Did you learn anything that you did not know?

5. Discuss your thoughts with your family and write your findings.

ADDITIONAL COMMENTS

Chapter 6

Use Good/Proper English and Good Grammar

Chapter 6 - Always use proper English when talking to anyone, especially your child. Avoid using slang words or profanity around your child during their formative years. Read to your child daily, encourage them to read a book as often as possible and develop a reading list for the summer with help from their teacher. Using good grammar and speaking well leads to the road to success. Encourage your child to read consistently, which will motivate your child to read and learn more.

Using good grammar is like having a good hygiene regimen and should be part of your daily life. Practice using good grammar. Good grammar allows you to speak and write properly, structure good sentences and have proper use of the English language. If needed, register in an English class at the local college, community center or take online courses. Speaking well and using good grammar is a plus for job interviews and exceling in life.

Are you familiar with **Code Switching**? Code Switching is the art of switching back and forth between two languages or dialects. People who are bilingual (i.e., speak two languages), often times speak interchangeably, switching back and forth from their main language or dialect to slang and back without skipping a beat or realizing they are code switching. Code Switching occurs more often during conversations instead of when writing. It also occurs when visiting or hanging out with friends. Have you ever noticed that some people speak in one manner at work and in a totally different manner when with family or friends? People who have not mastered the English language often use what is termed as "broken English" switching back and forth between their language and English. This is also considered Code Switching. The next time you hear bilinguals having a conversation, pay attention and try to identify if code switching occurs.

Personal Reflections – 6

1. Do you use slang when having a conversation with family and friends?

2. When was the last time you read a book?
   What was the name of the book and the author?

3. How often do you read a book?

4. What are your thoughts about this chapter?

5. Did you learn anything that you did not know?

6. Discuss your thoughts with your family and write your findings.

ADDITIONAL COMMENTS

Chapter 7

Dressing for Success and Interview Tips

Chapter 7 - This chapter covers items such as dressing for success Do's and Don'ts, and Interview Tips. Many of the items listed on the Do's and Don'ts List are common place and should be a no brainer, but if you have never been told or never read the information, you don't know. If practiced consistency, it will take little to no extra effort to perform or make the items listed common place in your life. Consider the following Do's and Don'ts on your road to success:

Don'ts

- Don't wear outrageously colored hair (i.e., purple, pink, blue etc.) to an interview.
- **Men and Women – Don't wear head-rags, bonnets, scarfs, hair rollers, shower caps or do-rags out in public.** This is a total **Disgrace**.
- Don't wear flip flops to an interview.
- Slippers are meant to be worn inside, not to the mall or shopping. Wearing slippers outside brings germs back into your home.
- Don't wear clothing with writing or slang on them.
- Don't wear dirty or un-ironed clothing
- Men – Don't wear Saggin pants. Always wear a belt. **Saggin spelled backwards is 'Niggas'. Notice that the 'g' has been dropped from sagging.** I wish all of the guys wearing saggin pants were aware of this. That alone should make someone want to stop wearing sagging pants.
- Women – Don't wear dresses or skirts too short. Remember

the **fingertip rule,** which means the length of your dress or skirt should not be shorter than your fingertips when your hands and fingertips are held to your sides.

- Don't chew gum at job interviews.
- Don't wear leggings to an interview or outside unless your bottom is covered. By all means wear the proper size.
- Men and Women - Don't wear overbearing fragrances.
- Don't wear gaudy jewelry.
- Don't show up without bathing, clipping/cleaning your nails, brushing your teeth, ironing your clothes and cleaning/polishing your shoes. Always be well groomed.
- Don't wear jeans to an interview (unless that is all you own) or to work unless permitted.
- **Men and Women – PLEASE Don't wear pajamas (PJs) outside of the home. PJs are meant to be worn at home and not to the mall and the grocery store.** This is **not a good look** and is tasteless.
- Don't wear party clothes to an interview.
- Men - Don't wear a cap/hat at the dinner table. Always remove your hat/cap upon entering a building.
- Don't text or talk on your phone while at an interview.
- Women - Don't wear the wrong size bra. Your bra should fit comfortably, with your breast fitting comfortably in the cup size and your back should not overflow the sides of the bra. If not sure of your correct bra size, go to a bra shop for proper measurements.

Do's

- Wear clothing that is clean, comfortable and wrinkle free.
- Wear simple jewelry for interviews.
- Layout your clothes the night before. Be prepared.
- Always polish or clean your shoes.
- Be on time for any appointment (i.e., interview or doctor's appointment etc.)
- Take multiple clean copies of your current resume in a folder to an interview.
- Men and Women - Do wear a dark suit when appropriate or a classic black jacket or black or brown slacks. If you do not own a suit or jacket, wear your best. Very nice clothes can be purchased at a second hand or thrift store.
- Men or Women - If you wear locs (i.e., natural hair), put your hair in a bun or ponytail for interviews or business meetings. Always maintain natural hair.
- Men and Women – If you are on a sports team, on game day always look your best. Never wear sweats for jogging gear.
- Remember to turn your cell phone off during an interview.
- Always look your best. Step out with a polished look.
- Men/boys always open and hold all doors for women/girls. At restaurants, pull the chair out when a women/girl attempts to be seated and assist her by pushing the chair in to the table. Doing this makes you a *Gentleman*.

Interview Tips

- Research the position you are interviewing for and practice your responses.
- Be prepared with a list questions about the position and the company.
- Dress for success and to impress. Follow the Do's and Don'ts.
- Bring 3 -5 copies of your current resume.
- Be ready to provide information about yourself, your current job, your strengths, your weaknesses and why you would be a good fit for the position.
- Arrive 15 minutes prior to the interview. Always arrive early.
- Silence your cell phone before entering the interview.
- Sit-up and maintain good posture.
- Do not chew gum.
- Be confident and remain calm.
- Be prepared to provide 3-5 references upon request.
- After the interview firmly shake everyone's hand and thank them for the interview.
- Follow-up with the Interviewer 2-3 days after the interview to express your interest.

Personal Reflections – 7

1. What does dressing for success mean to you?

2. Do you prepare your clothes the night before for school, church or work? Please explain.

3. Are you familiar with the Do's and Don'ts List?
   What is your opinion of each list?

4. What are your thoughts about this chapter?

5. Did you learn anything that you did not know?

6. Discuss your thoughts with your family and write your findings.

ADDITIONAL COMMENTS

Chapter 8

Resume Tips

Chapter 8 - Depending on your age, you may or may not have a resume. If you do not have a resume, it is very likely you have no work experience. If this is the case, develop a resume as soon as possible. When applying for a job, attach a resume with a job application if possible. The following fields should be included on a resume; name, address, phone number, an objective, high school or college, dates of attendance, major course work or discipline in high school or college, clubs, activities, memberships, awards, community service, internships and GPA.

For experienced workers, resumes should consist of your name, address, phone number, an objective, high school or college, dates of attendance, certifications, security clearances, memberships, awards, GPA, internships and past and present work experience with dates. It is very important to avoid and account for any gaps in time on your resume. For your convenience, there are several online resume templates and resume builders available to assist you in developing a resume. For high school and college students, with little to no work experience, it is a good practice to keep your resume to one page. For the more experienced person with work history, your resume should not be longer than two pages where possible. A properly written resume is precise, to the point with bulleted information and succinct. Avoid long essay type information on your resume. Keep your resume current with updated information. For more information, search online for resume templates.

<u>Resume contents:</u>

- Name, address, phone number and email address.
- Objective
- Certifications
- Awards
- Work Experience (In chronological order starting with current employment. If no work experience, enter dates for high school and college.)
- Education and GPA
- Skills/Capabilities
- Security clearances
- References (Include a statement 'References Available upon Request' at the end of your resume.)

Sample Resume:

Ginny Inovan
122 Best Street - Omaha, Nebraska 11111
333-345-5678 - Ginnyl@gmail.com

Objective:

To be able to apply the conceptual knowledge and skills acquired throughout my academic years in Computer Science.

Experience:

October 2018 – Present   Systems Engineer, DEEP Solutions

Responsible for designing, developing, and implementing test cases and test reports for a wide variety of products and processes. Duties include testing and evaluating new tools, processes, applications and software for operational.

Education:

Bachelor of Science in Computer Science – Onunu State University, May 2018, GPA 3.75

SKILLS AND CAPABILITIES:

JIRA, SIGINT Tools dealing with Metadata, Remedy, CASPORT, Beginners level training in SM7, Object-Oriented Programming (C#, Visual Basic, SQL & COBOL), Analysis, Design & Implementation, Management Information Systems, Project Management, Applied Information Technology, Business

References Available Upon Request

Personal Reflections – 8

1. Do you have a current resume?

   If not, how much effort would it take to update or make your resume current?

2. Does your resume follow the suggested tips?

3. What are your thoughts about this chapter?

4. Did you learn anything that you did not know?

5. Discuss your thoughts with your family and write your findings.

<u>ADDITIONAL COMMENTS</u>

Chapter 9

Cursive Writing

Chapter 9 - Cursive writing is a form of writing also known as script or longhand. This form of writing has become extinct in many of our schools today. Cursive or longhand writing is where letters are linked together to form words. Without this form of writing, our children will never know how to write their own signature and for some they will not be able to read historical documents. Did you know that many of our historical documents such as; birth records, death and marriage certificates, diaries and oldgovernments documents (i.e., the Bill of Rights and the Constitution etc.) are written in cursive writing? If cursive writing is no longer in your school's curriculum and you are interested in keeping it in your school or bringing it back into the schools, petition your local board of education through the PTA.

Some do not know the difference between manuscript and cursive writing and very often confuse the two. Manuscript is handwritten or printed words and cursive is free flowing letters linked together to form words.

Parents you can teach your child cursive writing. Start by purchasing a writing table with dotted lines or double spaced line tablets for your child to practice. Books with sample writings of cursive letters from A-Z upper case and lower case are also available, as well as practice books to learn how to do cursive writing. Remember practice makes perfect. Cursive writing samples from Regina's Tablet are below.

Sample - Cursive Alphabets in upper case A-Z and lower case a-z.

a B C D E F G H
I G K L M N O
P Q R S T U V W
X Y Z
a b c d e f g h i
j k l m n o p q r
s t u v w x y z
cat·dog· Regina··pop

Sample - Cursive Phrases

Apple of my eye.
See Jane go.
Bob and weave
It's kite day.
Up up and away.
Stop at the light.
Gone with the wind.
Go for it.

Sample - Cursive Signatures

John B. Doe
Sue E. Doe
J. B. Doe
S. E. Doe
John V. Hancock

Personal Reflections – 9

1. Do you know how to write in longhand or cursive writing? If not, would you like to learn how?

2. How often do you use cursive writing? What is cursive writing used for?

3. What are your thoughts about this chapter?

4. Did you learn anything that you did not know?

5. Discuss your thoughts with your family and write your findings.

ADDITIONAL COMMENTS

Chapter 10

Financial Literacy

Chapter 10 – Keeping track of your own money is the beginning of financial literacy. Learning to count money is a difficult task for many children. The earlier you introduce or start teaching the concept of counting money the easier it is to grasp. Purchase a money kit at the local craft or toy store. Identify the different denominations of coins and bills and start counting with your child consistently. You'll find that when a child learns to count their own money, leaning to count and keeping track of their own money is acquired very quickly.

The best way to get a child started early with learning about finances is by providing an allowance and allow them to keep track of their own money. This is a great way to help them get into the practice of saving by setting aside a portion of their allowance. Another early method in teaching a child to save their money is to take them to the bank to open a savings account. If possible, allow your child to assist with or complete the application. Encourage your child to deposit money into the account often. This is the beginning to learning the basics of finances.

Many fraternities and sororities offer workshops on financial literacy for children from 8-18 years as part of their service projects. You may also enroll your child in a class at the local Community Center. Many of the sessions are age and grade level appropriate. There are also many online age appropriate courses. A financial course can be beneficial in many ways. Many offer sessions on 'How to Manage Money?', 'Who Wants to be a Millionaire?', 'What is a Savings or Checking Bank Account and How it Works?', 'What is Credit?', 'What is a Credit Score?', 'How

Does a Credit Card Work?', 'How to Write a Check?' What is a Financial Advisor? Some sessions offer real life scenarios to better equip the students. There are also games available where children can learn about financial literacy. Don't delay.

Those fortunate enough to be employed who are married, single, single parents, in college or in need of tracking their finances, should always develop a budget to account for and keep abreast of their spending and expenses. Budgets can also be a vital tool for newlyweds in managing their finances. Establish a pattern for saving. Be in control of your finances. Be smart. Start saving while you are young. Find a financial planner that you are comfortable with to manage your finances. Develop a budget and stick to it. Signup for a 401K/Retirement Plan at work or open a Savings account as soon as possible. Every time you receive a raise, increase the percentage withheld from your paycheck. Long term this will be a huge financial benefit. There are so many additional benefits to establishing a 401K/Retirement Plan early, such as living comfortably upon retirement and being able to splurge for special activities and beyond.

Food for Thought: 1) Do you count your change when you make a purchase? If not, start counting your change and you will discover that some merchants will keep a penny or two every time. 'Why', you might ask? Simply because most people do not count their change. I discovered this many years ago and I was appalled that the same merchant attempted to short change me several times. This will happen to you too, if you don't stay woke; **2)** never, ever, ever, ever Co-sign on a loan for anyone. If they default on the loan for nonpayment, you are responsible and this could ruin your credit; **3)** every time you make a purchase from a candy bar to a sock, write it down to prevent overspending and to help you stay abreast of your weekly/monthly expenditures. This is plain and simple Budgeting 101 and it works.

Personal Reflections – 10

1. What does Financial Literacy mean to you?

2. Do you currently save money consistently?

3. What are your thoughts about this chapter?

4. Did you learn anything that you did not know?

5. Discuss your thoughts with your family and write your findings.

ADDITIONAL COMMENTS

Chapter 11

Writing a Check

Chapter 11 - In today's society, writing checks is becoming obsolete, but knowing how to write a check, the different fields on a check and the steps to write a check will be beneficial in the future. At some point in life you will need to know how to write a check. Writing a check is as easy as 1, 2, 3, but for many it is not as simple. A sample check is below. Note that every check has a pre-printed number. This number is important in case you ever need to reference the check. Let's get started. First, enter the date on the 'Date' line in the upper right corner, next enter the recipient's name in the 'Pay to the Order of' field, then enter the numerical dollar amount next to the '$' sign and then write the dollar amount in words. For example, if writing a check for $2.00, enter $2.00 next to the '$', then the written amount is Two and 00/100 for zero cents (Dollars is already listed). Finally, sign the check and enter the purpose for the check in the 'Memo' section.

Please beware that writing a fraudulent check is a crime and punishable by a fine and/or jail time. A picture of the sample blank check is listed below.

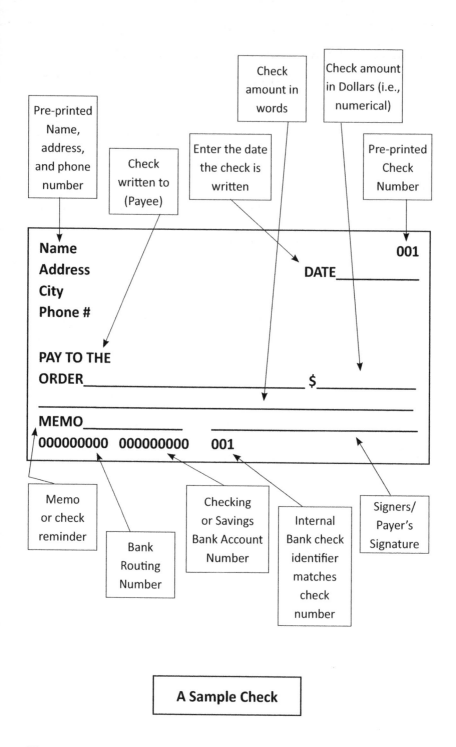

A Sample Check

Personal Reflections – 11

1. Do you write checks?

   How often do you write checks?

2. Do you prefer to write checks or to use a debit card?
   What is the advantage or disadvantage for both?

3. What are your thoughts about this chapter?

4. Did you learn anything that you did not know?

5. Discuss your thoughts with your family and write your findings.

ADDITIONAL COMMENTS

Chapter 12

Good Hygiene

Chapter 12 - *Hygiene* is defined as a condition or practice conducive to the preservation of health, as cleanliness. *Good Hygiene* starts with you and should be a part of your daily routine and is key to the prevention of health. Start by freshening up in the morning to include brushing and flossing your teeth, bathing and putting on clean clothes before you start your day. <u>Let me be clear; freshening up means washing your body, taking a bath or shower daily</u>. Athletes male and female, please take extra care of your bodies by showering daily, twice if necessary. Do not cut corners when caring for your body, give extra care to all of the areas. Males take extra care of your bodies and arm pits. Find a good anti-per spirant deodorant to use. Also, take extra care of your feet. Always keep your feet dry to prevent athlete's foot, which is a fungal infection of the foot, that affects male, female, boys and girls. Staying hydrated is also vital in maintaining good health by drinking plenty of water daily.

Maintaining good personal hygiene daily protects you and others and should become second nature. By always washing your hands after each bathroom visit, washing your hands before preparing or eating food and washing your hands after you sneeze are all good hygiene practices that must be a constant in your life. Always cover your mouth when you sneeze or cough. If possible, sneeze in the bend of your elbow, then wash your hands.

Many food borne illnesses occur because good hygiene is not practiced, hands are not washed and bacteria is passed during food preparation. Occasionally, food borne issues are related to improper food storage or preparation. Keeping food at the proper temperature is also vital in preventing issues. Food poisoning or Stomach Flu is a food borne illness and is directly related to contaminated food as the result of bacteria or parasites being passed in your food. Teach your child good hygiene practices early by showing them how to wash their hands, when to wash their hands, how to keep their nails clean and clipped and how to wash and keep their bodies clean. Children are never too young to learn. Teach your children early. Your total body hygiene has a direct connection to your total body health. Find and visit a doctor regularly. Take care of your body which is your temple. In addition to maintaining good hygiene, it is essential that you get sufficient rest and eat properly. *1 Corinthians 6:19* – "Do you know that your body is a temple of the Holy Spirit who is in you, whom you have received from God? You are not your own".

Menstrual Cycle (Females) is the recurring cycle of physiological changes in the uterus, ovaries, and other sexual structures that occur from the beginning of one menstrual period through the beginning of the next. Girls typically begin their menstrual cycle between the ages 8 – 14. Many health classes are offered in the public schools for girls as well as boys. There is plenty of literature at your local health clinic or doctor and information online regarding menstruation.

Young ladies should take extra care during their monthly *menstrual cycle* to ensure their body is kept clean and body odor is kept under control. Additional care may be required during this time of the month. Using tampons or pads properly is vitally important as well as **changing the used items in a timely**

fashion or at the recommended times to prevent complications, such as toxic shock syndrome. Special care should also be taken to properly dispose of the soiled items. Wrap the soiled items in tissue, paper towels, disposal bags or whatever is available and put the soiled item in another bag in the trash outside if possible. Soiled items can be very smelly, always double wrap the items. Proper disposal is very important to avoid unpleasant odors. If unsure of what to do when your menstrual cycle begins, talk to a responsible adult, a health care provider/doctor or school counselor for advice. Don't forget to wash your hands each time after changing tampons or pads and handling soiled items.

Birth Control is one of the many ways used to prevent pregnancy. There are many forms of birth control such as birth control pills, injections, patches, vasectomies, condoms for male and female, implants, and birth control devices (i.e., Intrauterine Devices (IUD), Diaphragm, Vaginal Ring etc). Men, women and teenagers be informed protect yourself against unwanted pregnancies and sexually transmitted diseases (STD). Practice safe sex. Birth control is a subject that is best discussed with a professional such as a school counselor, health teacher/instructor, a counselor/nurse at the local clinic or your healthcare provider/ doctor. Prevent unwanted pregnancies.

Be Smart, Protect Yourself.

Oral Hygiene should also be practiced and it the most important thing to maintain healthy teeth and gums. Brush and floss your teeth and use mouth wash after each meal, if possible. If not, brush and floss your teeth at a minimum once daily. Learn

71

how to brush and floss correctly. Good healthy teeth add to your overall health and well-being because it makes you feel good, clean teeth look good and no one in this world wants to see dirty teeth and a smelly breath. Find a dentist that you are comfortable with and visit your dentist regularly to keep your teeth and gums in good health and free from disease. Keep your tooth brush clean and replace it often. Did you know that bad teeth can lead to gum disease? All of your teeth can fall out and gum disease can kill you. Your oral hygiene also has a direct connection to your total body health.

Foot Hygiene or foot care is another part of your total hygiene regime. Keep your feet clean and dry at all times to prevent Athlete's foot which is caused by a fungus when your feet become damp and warm. Clip your toe nails regularly. During exercise and sports, wear socks at all times to keep your feet as dry as possible. Always dry your feet completely and between your toes after you bathe. If affordable, an occasional professional pedicure is a good way to maintain good foot health. If not, a home pedicure will suffice.

Personal Reflections – 12

1. What are your thoughts about all facets of good hygiene (i.e., body, oral, and feet)?

2. What would you do if you knew someone that does not practice good hygiene consistently?
   Is it a good idea to approach a person having hygiene problems? How would you handle the situation?

3. What are your thoughts about this chapter?

4. Did you learn anything that you did not know?

5. Discuss your thoughts with your family and write your findings.

ADDITIONAL COMMENTS

Chapter 13

Employment

Chapter 13 - One of our main sources for survival is being gainfully employed, preferably with a company that provides good benefits such as; medical and dental benefits, paid time off (PTO) more commonly known as vacation, a retirement plan and in some cases company stock. Being gainfully employed is a privilege. Employment is defined as the state of being employed, performing a service, or an occupation by which a person earns a living or income, an activity that occupies a person's time in return for an hourly wage (i.e., a non-exempt employee) or a salaried employee (i.e., exempt employee). The main difference between a non-exempt employee and exempt employee, is the non-exempt employee is paid overtime for every hour worked and the exempt employee is exempt from overtime pay and typically earns a higher pay or salary.

There are certain aspects of employment that many do not grasp, such as **Time Management** (i.e., being on time and using your time wisely during the day). Do not rely on others (i.e., your parents, family or a friend) to wake you up in the morning and for appointments. Be responsible. Get an alarm clock or use the alarm on your phone, set it and start your own pattern for time management. On most jobs, the start time is typically identified as a way of outlining the employees start time for employment. Many companies today have established a window between 2-4 hours (i.e., 6:00 am – 10:00 am), and the start time is at the employer's discretion, while others companies are more liberal and leave it totally up to the employee to identify their start time or arrival anytime during the 2-4 hour period known as the core hours. Regardless of the situation, establish a start time and be consistent. Inconsistency is a form of being irresponsible. Consistent attendance is also a form of being responsible and reliable. No work no pay. Another good practice is to plan your work week or your work day by making a schedule. If you work in an office, you probably have a computer and email. As part of the office suite of software on your computer, there is typically a calendar. Make use of the calendar by planning your week/day. List all of your daily/monthly tasks and meetings on the calendar. This is very beneficial in managing your time and does not leave room for idle time. Learn how to stay busy by managing your time. Don't be a slacker. Do The Work! Lying is a terrible thing.

Timecard fraud is another area for concern. Most technical employers require employees to complete their timecards at the end of each day, while service or blue collar employers require their employees to punch a time clock at the beginning and end of their work day. Many technical jobs allow their employees limited freedoms. Do not abuse the privilege of being able to come and go as you please. It is highly unethical to abuse your work hours/time. Timecard fraud occurs for several reasons, but the most common reasons occur when; the employee is absent from work frequently, the employee consistently comes to work late, leaves work early, takes long lunches without making up the time or takes multiple breaks during the day and lies about the number of hours worked on their timecard. This is Time Card Fraud. Timecard fraud is very serious can result in termination of employment or in some rare cases jail time or fines.

In today's workforce, many company's support projects that work with integrated product teams (IPTs) with support from various projects. It is vitally important that you are able to work in a team environment and get along with everyone on the team.

Application Tips – Before you begin your application, read the directions first, then go back to complete the application. Make sure you have all of the information necessary to complete the application and a current copy of your resume. Some applications can be completed online while others are completed manually using an ink pen. For applications completed manually, do a practice application before the final application is completed. The practice application is a way to ensure all of the fields are accurate and complete before the application is submitted and should be a simple transfer of information. Be as neat as possible, no erasures, complete all fields accurately with the correct information. Include work history in a chronological order, listing current employment first. Also, include job descriptions for your current and past employment, bulleted information works best, as well as 3-5 references. References should include one or two work related references and one or two personal references, with their name, address, phone numbers and the length of time you have known the reference.

Where possible, complete applications online. For online applications, the same tips (i.e., read the directions and complete all fields) for manual applications apply. Before submitting your online application, or any work performed online always check the spelling using Spellcheck to ensure all words are spelled correctly and verify all fields are complete.

Customer Service Jobs – One of my pet peeves is supporting a business by spending my money and being disrespected by an employee, by their display of a funky non business-like attitude. When you have a position that requires you to work with the public (i.e., service or blue collar jobs (non-technical jobs)), always put your best face and foot forward. Always wear a smile, say good morning and thank you to the customer for their business. **Keep the attitude at home.** If you do not want a service job working with the public, do not take the job and display your misery and BAD ATTITUDE. Some customers are difficult, but it is your job to maintain control and keep your attitude in check. Remember 'the customer is always right', **not really**, but that's the attitude you must always display at work even when it is not easy to do so. Be responsible at work, do not waste time gossiping, playing around or cracking jokes. Every job is important. Remember 'Professional is as Professional does'.

If customer service jobs are not for you, get an education so that you can secure a technical job. **DO NOT** go to work with an attitude disrespecting the business, the customer, and yourself. You are better than that. Remember your performance will be reviewed annually and a bad attitude and disrespect for customers will garner you a not so favorable review and possibly no raise.

Tips/Tipping - Tipping is common and is done when eating out at restaurants or at places that provide a service. A tip is usually how waiters, waitresses and service jobs make their money, because their bases salaries are usually very low and tips make up the rest of the salary. Many customers leave tips based on the service and attitude provided. Some waiters and waitresses must share a portion of their tips to a pool to be shared with the other support staff. Tips range for 15% - 25% with 20% being the average. Some other support or service jobs where tips enhance salaries are in the range of $1 - $10; nail salon attendant, hair stylist, parking attendant, sky caps, coat check, room service, and pizza delivery. Be responsible, do not skip out on the tip.

Business Sense – Having Business Sense is how an entrepreneur, customer, employee, employer or stakeholder deals with or handles business. Always have a discussion with the customer to document the requirements/specifications and the agreed upon expectations for the services to be provided. Negatively responding, poor time management, and bad attitudes all play an important role and can make or break a business. The old saying "Your word is your bond" means everything when in business. Whether you are in business for yourself or you work for someone else, if you schedule a time to arrive, you don't show up, you consistently arrive late or you agree to do a job/service and you don't perform the work as expected, this **sets the tone for a bad business relationship.** Things happen and sometimes you might be late, but pick-up the phone and inform the party of the situation. Do not text. Make it your business to talk to someone. Entrepreneurs, if you schedule an appointment or an arrival time and you are consistently late by any time more than 15 minutes, this is totally unacceptable and leaves very bad taste in the customer's mouth. This borders on a trust issue, creates a bad business relationship and the customer will likely not use your service again or refer you to their family or friends. Remember, everyone's time is valuable, not just yours. Always make every effort to do the work expected. A good business practice when performing a service, is to incorporate checkpoints or milestones with the customer along the way to ensure their expectations are being met. Many corporations have checkpoints in place for employee's performance, either monthly, mid-year or annually. When good business is practiced, businesses tend to flourish and are profitable. Where there is bad business sense or businesses are run hap hazardly, this is the beginning of the demise of the business and many times the businesses fold. *Titus 3:14:* - "And let our people too learn to set a **good example** in following honest occupations for the supply of their necessities, so that they may not live useless lives".

Personal Reflections – 13

1. Are you currently working?
   If so, how do you treat your employment?

2. Are you a professional in the way you handle your employment/job?

3. What are your thoughts about Time Management? Are you consistently late for appointments or events? If so, why?

4. Do you prepare at night for the next day? If not, why?

5. What are your thoughts about this chapter?

6. Did you learn anything that you did not know?

7. Discuss your thoughts with your family and write your findings.

ADDITIONAL COMMENTS

Chapter 14

Driving and Road Courtesy

Chapter 14 - Driving and road courtesy is high on the list next to safety. A courteous driver is a safe driver. Many times traffic bottlenecks can be avoided if drivers are courteous and allow other drivers to merge into their lanes during heavy traffic. Let people in, it won't kill you. Road rage is at an all-time high and streaming out of control. It is best to remain calm at all times while behind the wheel, because road rage incidents can escalate out of control so easily and lead to aggressive driving. A car is not a toy and should not be treated as such. **Do not drink and drive, text, apply make-up, eat or throw objects** at other cars while driving. Always remain attentive while driving. Throwing an object at another car in a misdemeanor is some states. Always keep calm and remain courteous. *Titus 3:2 –* "To malign no one, and to be peaceable and gentle, showing full consideration to everyone".

Parking a vehicle is another area that can be a major bone of contention when courtesy and respect is not practiced. Parking your car in a parking lot or garage is based on the honor system. Do you adhere to the honor system when waiting for a parking space? Always wait your turn when waiting for an available space. Never, never, never undercut someone waiting for a parking space ahead of you because it is convenient for you. This is disrespectful. **Don't do it!** Parking situations can easily escalate. If this happens to you, let it go. Keep calm and wait for the next available space. An altercation over a parking space is not worth it. Rise above the situation, turn the other cheek and let it go. It could cost you your life.

To report an aggressive driver, pull over dial 911 and provide the license plate number, the make, model and the color of the car and the direction in which the car is headed.

Personal Reflections – 14

1. Do you remain calm when driving?

2. Have you ever experience road rage?
    What was the outcome?

3. What are your thoughts about this chapter?

4. Did you learn anything that you did not know?

5. Discuss your thoughts with your family and write your findings.

<u>**ADDITIONAL COMMENTS**</u>

Chapter 15

A Balanced Diet and Exercise

Chapter 15 - Just a few brief words on diet and nutrition. Consumption of a balanced diet is the fuel required for your body to function daily. Consult your Doctor, dietitian or nutritionist to assist you in planning your food plan for a balanced diet that meets your dietary needs. Always eat three balanced meals per day along with exercise. Proper diet and nutrition to include proteins, carbohydrates and other nutrients and an active lifestyle is the key to success for a healthy you and your family. Pre-planned meals (i.e., meal prep) are also a key to success as well as recording everything you consume daily for accountability and staying on track. Meals prepared ahead of time play an important role in helping to stay on track. Limit the number of times that you eat out for lunch and dinner. Pack a lunch as often as possible. For dietary suggestions for balanced meal planning, remember to always consult a professional before you begin your journey. You can also research balanced diets and nutrition online. If you are on medications, PLEASE consult with your doctor before starting any eating plan.

The Food Pyramid, which you might remember from your health class in school is a pyramid shaped nutrition guide that provides recommended food consumption for each food group. The Food Pyramid is divided into **five major color coded groups**; grains (brown/orange), vegetables (green), fruits (red), milk (blue), and proteins (purple). For balanced meals, try as much as possible to incorporate the recommended or appropriate selections from each food group daily.

The Food Pyramid five major food groups;

- **Brown/**Orange - Grains (whole grains and refined grains)
- Green - Vegetables and legumes (beans) fresh, frozen and canned
- **Red** - Fruit (apples, oranges, bananas, berries etc.) fresh, frozen and dried
- Blue - Milk, yogurt and cheese
- **Purple** - Proteins (meat, poultry, fish, seafood, nuts, seeds, tofu, eggs)

In addition to a balanced diet, include at least a minimum of 30 – 45 minutes of exercise or walking 3-5 times weekly. If you have never exercised and want to start working out on a consistent basis, **start slow** and make sure you have comfortable clothes and the right shoes to avoid injury before you begin. Next identify, the type of exercise you plan to incorporate and set a small goal to get started. You may also consider a gym membership, a workout facility or a physical trainer to assist you with this endeavor. Many local community center's offer classes such as Yoga, Zumba, Jazzercise and routine exercise classes. Remember, to stay hydrated by drinking plenty of water and sports drinks. Sodium, potassium and other minerals are lost during exercising and sports, but can be replenished with sports drinks. When playing a sport or exercising, your body perspires/sweats more than normal and the potential for injury is higher if not properly cared for by stretching and staying hydrated. As always, consult your doctor or a health care professional before you begin any program. Be committed for success.

Personal Reflections – 15

1. Do you eat a balanced diet from the Pyramid Group daily?

   What do you eat for breakfast?

   Lunch?

   Dinner?

2. Do you exercise consistently? If so, how often?

   What form of exercise?

3. What are your thoughts about this chapter?

4. Did you learn anything that you did not know?

5. Discuss your thoughts with your family and write your findings.

ADDITIONAL COMMENTS

Chapter 16

How to Thread a Needle

Chapter 16 - Threading a needle is a simple but lost art, but can be done in a few simple steps; **1)** Select the thread of choice, **2)** Cut a piece of thread long enough for your project about 20 inches, **3)** Ensure the tip to be threaded is even and pointed, if not, clip the end at an angle with the scissors, **4)** Moisten the tip of the thread and gently guide through the eye of the needle, **5)** Once the thread is through the eye, pull the thread through and match the two ends of the thread and securely make a knot by wrapping the two ends of the thread around your finger and forming a knot. Threading a needle can be difficult for some, when this happens there is a tool called a Needle Threader used to get the thread through the eye of the needle. There are also Self Threading Needles available to assist in threading a needle, simply loop one end of the thread and slide the thread over a slot in the needle and like magic the needle is threaded. You are now ready to sew on a button or hem a garment. Practice makes perfect. It's like riding a bike, once you master the craft you will never forget it. It's Easy Peasy! Who knows you might be the next High fashion designer.

Personal Reflections – 16

1. What are your thoughts about this chapter?

2. Did you learn anything that you did not know?

3. Discuss your thoughts with your family and write your findings.

ADDITIONAL COMMENTS

Chapter 17

Thank You Note Cards

Chapter 17 - Have you ever received a graduation gift, birthday gift, retirement gift, shower gift, or you received help from a friend/family or someone performed a good deed/favor for no particular reason? If so, did you send a thank you note? This is another one of my pet peeves. While **it is not** mandatory to send a thank you, it is a common courtesy to say 'Thank you'. Sending a thank you note is typically not expected, but what better way to let the giver know you are grateful for the gift or service and the gift is appreciated. Verbally saying thank you is good, but make it a habit of saying thank you by sending handwritten or pre-printed thank you note cards, emails, online cards or handwritten letters. **Do not send a text** or a verbal message by someone else. This is unacceptable and very poor taste. In today's technical society, handwritten or online cards are both acceptable and appreciated. It is always best to send thank you notes immediately after receipt of a gift or service, otherwise, the thought of sending one might be forgotten. One to two weeks after receipt of the gift is customary for sending a thank you note.

With children, start this practice early. Write a sample thank you note for them including the giver's name and the gift received. Allow your child to write the words in the note themselves to make it personal. It will soon become common place and they will remind you to send a thank you note. For small children, allow them to be creative and create their own thank you notes and even color them. They will love it!

When multiple gifts are received, make a list of all gifts tangible or monetary and the giver's name. Check each recipient off the list when the thank you note has been sent.

Personal Reflections – 17

1. What are your thoughts about this chapter?

2. Did you learn anything that you did not know?

3. Discuss your thoughts with your family and write your findings.

ADDITIONAL COMMENTS

Chapter 18

How to do Laundry or Wash Clothes

Chapter 18 - One of the most important things to do before washing clothes is knowing how to prepare your clothes for washing. Washing clothes can be done in just a few easy steps; **1)** Separate clothes into separate loads by color or material (i.e., white, colored, towels, bulky or delicate). Each load should be washed separately, **2)** Set the load/capacity size for the washer (i.e., small, medium or large), **3)** Set the water type, hot, cold or warm. White clothes are typically washed in hot/warm water with a bleach or whitener and dark clothes are typically washed in warm or cold water, depending on your preference and type of material, **4)** Wash cycles vary depending on the clothes being washed and the length of the wash cycle (e.g., the delicate or short cycle is used for delicate items such as lingerie or underwear), **5)** Next put in the washing detergent/powder of choice and the clothes being washed. Note that today washing detergents comes in different forms; pods, liquids and powder, **6)** Fabric softener can be added to the wash cycle or a fabric sheet with softener can be added to the dryer once the clothes have completed the wash cycle, and **7)** After your clothes have been washed and dried, make the final step a habit by folding your clothes and putting them away. This is a great opportunity to get your children involved and a great way to teach them how to do laundry. Folding your clothes immediately after drying them can in many instances eliminate the need for ironing. After your clothes have been washed and put away, another good practice is to prepare your clothes for the next day.

'Have you ever seen a clothes line or clothes pins, which

are both rarely seen and a thing of the past'? Many third world countries still use clothes lines and clothes pins today. We now have washers, dryers and laundry mats. No more having to hang clothes outside in the freezing cold or blazing heat. We are truly blessed.

Personal Reflections – 18

1. What are your thoughts about this chapter?

2. Did you learn anything that you did not know?

3. Discuss your thoughts with your family and write your finding

ADDITIONAL COMMENTS

Chapter 19

Basic Safety Tips

BASIC SAFETY TIPS

- ✓ Talk to your child about the importance of safety in your everyday life.
- ✓ Hold a small child's hand when out in public and before crossing the street.
- ✓ Always look both ways before crossing the street. Cross in the Pedestrian crosswalk.
- ✓ When walking on streets or roads, always walk on the side facing traffic. Parents when walking, keep your child on the inside away from traffic.
- ✓ At home, create a family escape plan in case of a fire and discuss it with the family.
- ✓ Teach your child fire safety. Tell them not play with matches or the stove.
- ✓ Never leave an unattended pot on the stove. Always make sure the handle of a pot is not in the reach of a child. Turn the handle toward the back of the stove.
- ✓ Never leave an unattended candle burning.
- ✓ Discuss car safety, the importance of always buckling your seat belt and keeping your hands inside of the car when the window is open.
- ✓ Do not post personal information on social media; Facebook, Twitter and Instagram. Never post derogatory information which could affect your current or potential employment.
- ✓ Teach your child/children not talk to strangers.
- ✓ Keep poisonous and dangerous items out of the reach of

children.

- ✓ Always wash your hands after using the restroom and before each meal.
- ✓ Always cover your mouth when you sneeze, then wash your hands.
- ✓ For small children, cover all electric outlets in your home and keep cords out of reach.
- ✓ Do not drink and drive.
- ✓ Do not text and drive.
- ✓ Do not apply makeup and drive.
- ✓ Be engaged in the daily lives of your children and family. Be informed.

Personal Reflections – 19

1. What are your thoughts about this chapter?

2. Did you learn anything that you did not know?

3. Discuss your thoughts with your family and write your findings.

ADDITIONAL COMMENTS

Chapter 20

Cell Phone Etiquette

Chapter 20 – Cellular (Cell) Phones also known as mobile phones are one of the many wonders of today's technology. Cell phones allow users to make and receive calls, take pictures, edit pictures, and make videos and much, much more. Technology is constantly changing and phones today are referred to as Smartphones. There are 1000's of Apps (i.e. Applications) that have been created to support these phones, from games, maps, GPS, clocks, karaoke and more. In a world with all of this technology, cell phone etiquette is necessary. Listed below are just a few tips for cell phone etiquette. Many young and old are blessed to have a cell phone, but most do not adhere to any cell phone etiquette. Please respect others when using your phone.

➤ Turn your cell phone off in meetings, dinner, restaurants, medical offices, church, school, movies, and public places.
➤ No texting while driving.
➤ Avoid texting in public places.
➤ Turn your cell phone off when in a store making a purchase. Do not talk on your cell phone while making a purchase.
➤ No loud talking. Your conversation is 'your conversation and should be private' and is not meant for everyone to hear or public consumption.
➤ Your speaker phone should be used in private. Again not for public consumption.
➤ Hands free phone equipment should be used while driving.

Personal Reflections - 20

1. What are your thoughts about this chapter?

2. Did you learn anything that you did not know?

3. Discuss your thoughts with your family and write your findings.

ADDITIONAL COMMENTS

Chapter 21

Your Civic Duty

Chapter 21 – It is an honor and a privilege to be a citizen of the United States of America. As citizens of the United States of America, we are obliged with certain rights and charged with performing certain responsibilities such as paying your state (if applicable) and federal taxes to government, voting, jury duty when called to serve, volunteering, and being a law abiding citizen. Personally, I consider belonging to a church as part of my civic duty and being a productive citizen in my community, but you might feel differently. There are many more civic obligations, but the items listed are the basic civic responsibilities.

Depending on the age requirement for your state, make sure you are registered to vote and encourage your child to register to vote as soon as the age requirement is met. The Board of Elections in most states offers workshops/classes to teach the voting and election process and civic duties. When you go vote, some polling places will allow you to bring your child with you when you vote. This is a great experience for a young child and it gives them something to look forward to. When your child becomes of age, take your child to register to vote at the earliest opportunity. It is our civic duty as a citizen to vote. **'YOUR'** vote could make the difference. Impress upon your child the importance of voting and that every vote counts. There are many other civic duties. For more information regarding Civic Engagement/Duty, contact your local Board of Elections.

Personal Reflections - 21

1. What is your civic duty as a citizen?

2. Do you know where to get information regarding your civic duty?

3. Are you registered to vote?

4. What are your thoughts about this chapter?

5. Did you learn anything that you did not know?

6. Discuss your thoughts with your family and write your findings.

ADDITIONAL COMMENTS

Chapter 22

Conclusion

Chapter 22 Conclusion - Because of my love for family, this is why I poured out my heart in writing this book. I was raised with the basic skills and exposed too much in life. Seeing the youth of today lacking in so many areas, I decided to share my knowledge because **they don't know**. We are losing each generation, and it is so obvious they are lacking the basic skills for becoming productive adults.

To help strengthen the family bond, build healthy relationships and boundaries, a few small changes in the family dynamics can make the difference. Start by establishing daily family times, set aside a time each day to talk and listen to your child, eat dinner together, ask your child about their day at school and share your day with the family. Learn to communicate and listen to your family, and finally, allow your child to be themselves by expressing their feelings to help build their self-esteem and develop wholesome individuals. Let us turn the tide from **'They Don't Know'** and keep the fire burning by passing the torch forward with the basic skills of life to our pre-teens, teenagers, young adults and parents, so that they will be **'In the Know'**. Change begins with you. Please don't 'Go along to get along or fake until you make it'. Be informed, ask questions. **Knowledge is power**. It's okay to ask questions. If you don't know ask someone, seek or research the answer. This book is a good initial resource and a jumpstart for many who are lacking basic knowledge and are eager to learn. It also has several good topics for dinner time conversations with family and friends. Remember 'It takes a village to raise a family' and 'Each one teach one'. For you are responsible for you and your family's survival.

Matthew 25:21 – "His lord said unto him, well done, *thou* good and **faithful servant**: thou hast been **faithful** over a few things, I will make thee ruler over many things: enter thou into the joy of thy lord".

Personal Reflections - 22

1. Would you recommend this book to family and friends? If so, why?

2. What are your thoughts about this chapter?

3. Did you learn anything that you did not know?

4. Discuss your thoughts with your family and write your findings.

ADDITIONAL COMMENTS

SPECIAL ACKNOWLEDMENTS

A special thank you to my husband Gleason and daughter Glenna for always standing by me with their full love and support. Without you this would not be possible. Also, a special thank you to my big sister Marlene Shaw Fullilove and a dear friend and sorority sister Eureka McAfee for their positive words of encouragement. Thanks to my friend Joyce Myrick Brooks for the photography.

About the Author

Regina Shaw Small grew up in Memphis Tennessee and was blessed to be raised by both parents Alonzo and Thelma Shaw both deceased. From early childhood, Regina was always quiet, but very creative and inquisitive. Although very shy, she accepted Christ early in life and has led a God fearing life. Recognizing her shyness, her Mom put her in many activities which encouraged her to want to do more from piano lessons, Brownie's, Girl Scouting all the way to senior level, Jr. and High School marching and concert bands, Jr. and Sr. church choirs, member of the Sunshine Band, Baptist Training Union (BTU), various social clubs in school, the community and more. While in elementary school, she was the backup pianist at the local funeral home when the regular pianist could not be there...Whew! She loved doing new things as well as to travel. Every summer from the age of seven Regina and a couple of her siblings went to overnight camp for two weeks. During her teen years she traveled to Chicago a few times to bring her nieces and nephews to Memphis for the summer to visit. This was always an adventure. A teenager traveling with five children on the train.

She received her B.S. degree in Elementary Education from Langston University, Langston Oklahoma, which is the last Historically Black College and University (HBCU) before you head west. While her teaching career was short lived, her career took a sudden turn toward engineering, where she spent her career as a systems engineer for more than forty years. Regina loved her new career, where her leadership and meticulous detailed work habits were recognized early. She was promptly rewarded for her efforts and elevated to lead positions and on to Management. She enjoyed training new test engineers how to perform testing properly using the System Integration and Test Methodology and how to become good test engineers. If there was a problem to be found in a system, Regina could find it. For many years, she travelled to California, to train new test engineers to the test process. The bulk of her career was spent with the Northrop Grumman Corporation with over 20 plus years of service, followed by BAE, Raytheon and retiring from Leidos Corporation in 2018.

Since retirement, she has continued her busy schedule as an active member of Kettering Baptist Church Legacy Center, Delta Sigma Theta Sorority, Inc., Langston University National Alumni Association (LUNAA), a volunteer with So Others Might Eat (SOME) and a founding member of the Women in the Circle (WIC) Prayer Group. Regina has been a member of Delta Sigma Theta Sorority, Inc. for the past 49 years, where she has continuously volunteered her time. She will celebrate 50 years as a Golden Delta in 2020. Life has been good and with God's continued Grace and Mercy, she will continue this journey. **John 14:15** – "If you love me, you will keep my commandments".

After years of seeing the demise of family units and pondering over the continual loss of basic skills by our younger generation, she decided to pen this book **'They Don't Know'**. Who knows where this book might land or end up, but her prayer is that it will be a blessing to someone. Just think, this could be the beginning of a series of self-help books. Stay tuned. Love ya!

Regina S. Small

My favorite scripture..........

Isaiah 40:31

"But those that wait on the Lord will renew their strength, they will mount up with wings like eagles, they will run and not grow weary, they will walk and not faint".

NOTES

NOTES

NOTES

NOTES

NOTES

Made in the USA
Middletown, DE
06 June 2020